T♥SWIFT
1989
13

FOR THE SWIFTIES!

Title: *1989 and Beyond: The Life of Taylor Swift*
Names: Higgins, Kaela - author | Babel, Emily - illustrator

1989 AND BEYOND

THE LIFE OF TAYLOR SWIFT

ERAS OF THE BOOK

On December 13, 1989, Scott and Andrea Swift welcomed a baby girl into the world. They named her Taylor after James Taylor, a famous singer and songwriter.

Taylor grew up in a little town in West Reading, Pennsylvania with her parents and her little brother, Austin. She also had two cats, Indy and Eliehsen, who didn't like anyone but Taylor!

Taylor and Austin grew up in a home filled with love and joy. The Swift family traveled to new places, had fun outside, and read books together.

Christmastime was Taylor's favorite time of the year when she was a child. She loved spending time with her family, exchanging presents, decorating for the holiday season, and playing in the snow.

But what made the holiday even more magical was that her family lived on a **Christmas tree farm!**

As a kid, Taylor had an active imagination. She made up fairy tales, stories, and wrote poetry. She knew every Disney song by heart. One day, she discovered a record by a country music star named LeAnn Rimes. From then on, she only wanted to listen to country music!

When Taylor was 9, she took acting and vocal lessons. Then, she performed in musical theater. She loved to sing and perform in front of audiences, but something was missing. Taylor knew she could be more.

One day she watched a documentary about country music superstar Faith Hill, and it clicked.

She wanted to write and sing her country music, and she wanted to **be a star!**

Her favorite superstars got their start in Nashville, Tennessee so 10-year-old Taylor begged her parents to take her. She knew what she needed to do; she just needed to get there.

And finally, it happened! A year later, Taylor, Austin, and their mom went to Nashville for spring break. They drove up and down a street lined with music recording studios and businesses called Music Row. Taylor went door to door with CDs she made of her singing covers of her favorite country songs.

To Taylor's disappointment, everyone rejected her, but it didn't slow her down. Everyone in that town wanted to become a star too, so she thought to herself, *I need to figure out a way to be different*.

She needed to be a
guitar-picking singer and songwriter.

She came home and immediately started guitar lessons with a local musician. She practiced for four hours every day after school and six hours on weekends. She played until her fingers bled, and then she bandaged them up and kept on playing! With her guitar teacher's help, she wrote her first song.

Taylor performed her songs at local events. She sang at ballgames, coffee shops, and festivals—anything to get seen.

She did a lot in her hometown, but it wasn't enough. She needed to go where the Dixie Chicks, Dolly Parton, and Shania Twain got their start. She had to go back to Nashville.

Taylor's parents had no doubt she could reach her dreams. When Taylor turned 13, the Swift family said goodbye to West Reading, Pennsylvania, and moved to a town near Nashville, so Taylor could get her start.

Right away, Taylor got a record deal. RCA Records signed her! Her dreams were coming true!

But the record label didn't want her to write her own songs. They wanted her to sing other people's songs. For Taylor, writing songs was just as important as singing them. But because she was young, the record label thought she should wait to put out her own album until she was older.

Taylor disagreed. She knew she was capable of more than they gave her credit for. At the age of 14, she performed at Nashville's Bluebird Café. She sang songs by other singers, but she also sang a couple of her own. Her setlist included "Songs About You," "Me and Britney," and "Beautiful Eyes." The crowd loved her!

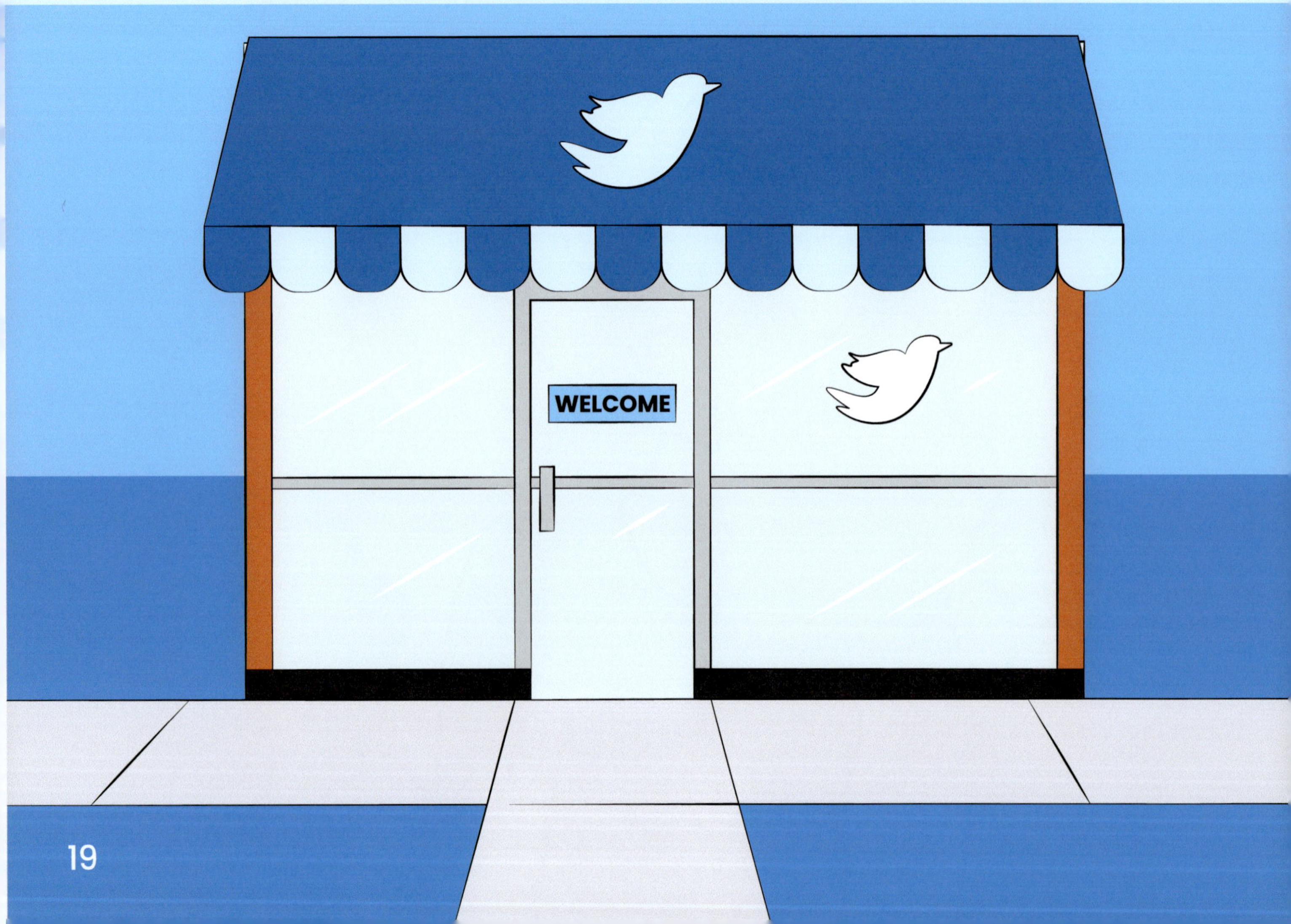

Afterward, a man approached her. He was a music executive forming a new record label and he wanted to sign Taylor!

Less than two years later, Taylor released her first single, "Tim McGraw." The song became a **top 10 hit** on the country charts! She couldn't believe it every time she heard it on the radio.

Taylor's debut album, *Taylor Swift*, came out later that year. It featured songs like "Picture to Burn," "Teardrops on My Guitar," and "Our Song." It sold more than two million copies! Taylor was so excited!

TAYLOR
SWIFT

At 18, she released her second album, *Fearless*.

This album made her famous, with songs like "You Belong With Me" and "Love Story." It became the top-selling record of the year. Taylor was a country music star, just like she dreamed! That year, she went on **her first concert tour** and captured the hearts of millions. The world fell in love with her.

FEARLESS

Taylor was a hard worker. Even though she achieved her dreams, she kept going. She always knew she could do more. She kept writing songs and putting out hit albums. Taylor **wrote and co-produced every song** on *Speak Now*, her third album.

This album is special to Taylor. She made tracklist after tracklist, obsessing over the right way to tell the story.

Taylor was a fantastic storyteller. Her songs told stories that many people relate to. Some people said her songs capture a feeling they had but never knew how to describe.

Many people told Taylor she wouldn't be able to achieve her dream. Girls at her school made fun of her for trying. Adults told her she wasn't unique or special enough. But never say never to Taylor Swift.

Two years after *Speak Now*, Taylor released *Red*.

She wrote it while she was becoming an adult, grappling with leaving behind her teen years. Taylor chose the color red because that's the color she associates with feelings like **heartbreak, love, passion, and anger**—all emotions Taylor experienced in her relationships in her early twenties.

RED

Taking risks is vital to Taylor so at age 24, she tried something new. Instead of country music, she recorded **her first pop album** called *1989*.

It was the best-selling album of that year!

1989

Three years later, Taylor released *Reputation*.

At this time in her career, Taylor dealt with the pressures of being in the public eye. Many people judged her music and said unkind things about her.

For Taylor, this album was about **finding love** through all the noise and how it makes you feel when people say things about you that aren't true.

REPUTATION

In 2019, Taylor released *Lover*.

She described her seventh album as a “love letter to love, in all of its maddening, passionate, exciting, enchanting, horrific, tragic, wonderful glory.” It was her first album after she departed from Big Machine Records, and **it went platinum!**

LOVER

Only a year later, Taylor released two sister albums, *Folklore* and *Evermore*, in five months. Instead of another pop album like her fans were expecting, Taylor's eighth and ninth albums were **indie folk**.

FOLKLORE

Unlike her previous albums, which were all based on her own life, these songs were about **fictional characters and told stories**, much like the ones she used to make up when she was a kid. Her fans loved it!

Taylor's album, *Midnights*, was released in late 2022.

Midnights was music written in the middle of the night throughout Taylor's life. "It's a journey through terrors and sweet dreams," Taylor said.

MIDNIGHTS

Today, Taylor is loving the life she's built for herself. Not only is she an international superstar, but she's a proud cat mom! She has three cats—Meredith Grey, Olivia Benson, and Benjamin Button.

Taylor has never been shy about making her cats part of her personality, and her fans love her all the more for it.

Meredith Grey

Now, Taylor has over 200 songs. She has one of the largest fan bases in the world. Even people who don't listen to her songs find her inspirational and brilliant. She paved the way for young female artists in the industry and continues to inspire young girls and women everywhere!

WHAT WILL SHE DO NEXT?

13
T♥SWIFT
1989

Printed by Libri Plureos GmbH in Hamburg,
Germany